A Wren

A Wren

poems by
Ger Killeen

Best Wishes,
Ger Killeen

Winner of the 1989 Bluestem Award

The Bluestem Press
Emporia State University
Emporia, Kansas

Acknowledgments

Some of these poems first appeared in the following publications: *New Irish Writing, Sparrow Poetry Pamphlet #56, Tocsin.*

Copyright 1989 by Ger Killeen

Design by Christopher Howell

Publication of this book was made possible in part by a grant from the Emporia State University Endowment Office.

Library of Congress Cataloging-in-Publication Data

Killeen, Ger, 1960-
    A Wren: poems / by Ger Killeen
    p. cm. — (The Bluestem Award)
    I. Title.   II. Series.
    PR6061.I35W7   1989
821'.914—dc20   89-18121

ISBN 1-878325-00-0 paper
      1-878325-01-9 cloth

Published by Bluestem Press, English Department, Emporia State University, Emporia, Kansas 66801

For Kate

"But the race of birds was created out of innocent light-minded men, who, although their minds were directed toward heaven, imagined, in their simplicity, that the clearest demonstration of the things above was to be explained by sight."
(*Plato*, 'Timaeus')

Contents

I. The Old Country

Wishes /3
Ghosts /4
My Father Shaving /5
Searching for Fireflies /6
The Woodsavers /7
Gulls /8
Les Fleurs de Nuit /9
Shaddimuddies /10
My Father's Angels /11
Caryatids /12
The Holy Well /13
A Folk Saying /14
Haystacks /15

II. Masque

Scrimshaw /19
The Catch /20
Ephiphanies /21
Rewind /22
Trapping /23
Tale /24
Without Design /25
Talking with Lions /26
Remembrance /28
Night Swimming /29
Jealousy /30
An Honest Lie /31
Tristia /32
Evolution Prayer /33
Meditation on an Incomplete Poem of Sappho /34
She /36
The Circulation of Light /37
No-Man /39
Webs /40

III. West

Redwoods /43
Anishinabemowin /44
In Light of Kansas /45
Home Sickness /47
Mrs. America /48
The Impersonators /49
Whales in October /50

IV. A Wren

A Wren /55
At the Black Edge /57

I

The Old Country

Wishes

A wish that I can get it true for you —

Snow bared the black lines of hedges in thorn.
The river stiffened like a swan's white neck
and every sound was like bone splintering
through the thick silence and the long skinless
fingers of the reeds, though it was only
ribbon flickering black against a door.

And I know that deep in your city you
have felt this too: the hard echoing
of the bell, and church voice wavering with
the slow candle; shuffle of feet on stone.

And perhaps within us too is harshness
of hill and monument, for pain only
brings our wishes that we can get it true.

Ghosts

In my grandfather's time everyone wore
grim clothes and black hats, went to funerals
wakes and weddings in grand carriages dragged
by horses with long backs and nodding plumes;
faces in an album he matched for me with names.

But grandfather, why in that museum
of your laughs would you not let them linger?
They were ghosts no story of yours
could banish to a photograph.
How else could they leap at me day and night out of

windows and hallways and streetlamps' shadows?
They were ghosts and you knew it.
Is there any other reason why
now every night you come to my bedside
and whisper in the dark like a terrible thing?

My Father Shaving

I'd watch him make the razor rasp
across his sudsy, stony face.
The sound was crisp as footsteps
through fields which frost has stiffened white.

A slip, and blood would blossom out,
a crocus pushing through a March snow;
was that, I thought, how faces got
their lines, was that how men grew old?

He'd shut his eyes and rinse his face.
Straggles of soap would thaw away;
over the rim of the sink I'd see
a scree of beard whirl around the drain.

Searching for Fireflies

Searching for fireflies I came upon all
kinds of unexpected darknesses —
the dark moans of contentment wintering
in the warm corners of haysheds,
the stiff residue of bushes blown
out like candles, and dark thoughts
coiled inside my own dark head. Searching
for fireflies I never found, I discovered
the white flesh-flash of a coupling
in the shifting shadows of steaming horses,
the snarling fires of a hobo camp
where no one sang, and lights
in the trees like nests. Now, knowing
things like the habitats of fireflies
and why I couldn't have seen what I saw,
I still see eruptions of light;
and just as Pascal sewed the word *fire*
inside his shirt, I find fireflies
in my pockets that burn to speech,
my lips still blazing in amazement.

The Woodsavers

Tell me something of what I've lost I told
the river flooded and much broken wood
floating fast. Surely you know what it is, they said,
the one pushing the other on the mud.

But I was a child at the last high wind,
know nothing of stormwater's ways. I saw
once a shining moorhen in the rushes dead,
deep years away; it was strange even then.
Yet they seemed not to hear, pushed inside me
fragments of voices by the other bank
and hands from a boat holding branches tight
against the rough tugging of the fastflow:
They were the woodsavers, called out to me
louder than any shouting of thunder.

Gulls

Climbing the walls of the asylum
we used to watch them pass,
eyes like holes in their white faces,
their slow voices; it made us laugh.

That was before we saw the man
who spoke up to us, moving his fingers
like soft feathers, revealing secrets
of signs in the land and sky.

Things to be remembered, he said,
and that was why we watched
with a strange fear when gulls,
driven by a storm,

stood like statues on the roof.
We understood at last
why the man said they had voices
and called their black heads cowls.

Les Fleurs de Nuit

If it were light I think the air would be
yellow with smell and bee-flight's ecstacy.
But, God, the dark is so much savagery
I hope this world has not been made for me.

Morning's red roses stand rigid with night,
retracted into a line of knuckles,
so stiff I think they're not alive, so still
they make me calm and quiet, and then

the fist between the eyes with the rising
of a hungry sound: deep in the chambers
of the flowers' black hearts the encrusted
greenfly gather into choruses and sing.

Shaddimuddies

One or two will always manage
to reach the cool, white heart
of a cabbage without leaving
a trace, or maybe they happen there
as pearls happen, secreted
in the innermost whorls, live births
as yet unaccomplished by oysters.

Sometimes you will find a pair
sealed to each other like lips, and
then there is surely a folk-tale
to explain why a prince and princess
burst to bits from passion or anger, mouths
tightened forever into silence,
eyeballs glazed brown into blindness.

And as children we chanted to them:
"Shaddimuddy, Shaddimuddy,
Come out of your hovel,
And we'll build you a palace
For all your trouble",
and some would slide cautiously
to our hands from under a broad leaf.

But other meanings are connected
to them, depending on whether you call them
Shaddimuddies, or Helices, or snails;
what name would it take, I wonder,
to work on them like a kiss and lure
into human forms again the young princess

and the prince bright with a new wisdom?

My Father's Angels

My father's angels
dropped to earth
like those of Tintoretto, heavy-limbed
and muscular as farm boys
saving the summer hay. And in his tales
they needed to be that way,
rescuing saints and ships at sea
and Spanish nuns from the Communists
in 'thirty-three. My father's angels
kept the world
on course for Paradise, and when
the gutters gushed with blood
in Derry and Belfast his angels
came and fell down on their knees,
rifles levelled and faces masked.
My father's angels
were angels through and through;
everything happened
like his favorite saint, Augustine,
says: When angels turn
their attention to the world of man
the nighttime falls. I heard
the darkness slam.

Caryatids

The Palace Ballroom was the ear of the storm.
The rain's virtuoso drum-roll on the green,
corrugated, metal roof cannoned through
The Walls of Limerick, The Siege of Ennis,
and other battles of the sexes.

A change of instruments brought a change of plan:
Little Arrows buzzed from two black amps
to the left and to the right; it was tough
to avoid being hit by the flailing elbows
of men who were used to pushing cows around.

But a lightning flash during *The Hokey Pokey*
cast everything into darkness and silence.
The women's dresses swished like tails in a byre,
and when the lights came on again, here and there,
women, continuing the last dance, stretched

their arms above their heads, as if holding off
apocalypse. At the end of the night
the band thundered *The Soldiers' Song*
to the crowd at attention, singing its heart out,
and then their cheering brought the house down.

The Holy Well

A half-circle of rough-cut stones and a few
foot-high pillars smooth at the top from years
of hands mark out the prescribed kneeling place
where you may drink and pray or simply look
down into the water. A thick canopy
of fuchsia gives everyone a crown of stars.

People have left there sky-blue ribbons,
pictures of Jesus, plaster Virgins, and crosses
with rosary beads looped around their arms.
I have watched farmers kneel for hours, their heads
clasped between their hands as if they were trying
to squeeze an answer out of their reflections.

I, too, have gone there, trying to rid myself
of despair, thoughts of my life's futility.
There were times when I would have given my soul
for someone to sever my body from my head
and let me dance for once unfettered
by a gravity of my own creation.

But even despair is not fatal: You drop
your questions like rocks into a well,
only now you call it a poem, and because
it comes from somewhere you don't understand
and looks to be bottomless, your questions
change from yourself to ones concerning

the well's or the poem's efficacy.
And in an act of faith you may kneel
on stones someone cut centuries ago,
drink from the water and make the required
offering of an image, expecting
no cures, but compelled to return again.

A Folk Saying

Jack never understood the ways
of a world that rewarded
head-work more than the work of the hands.
We'd lean together
against the wall around his fields
of barley and potatoes
discussing the weather
and politics, until,
with a half-irritated shrug,
he'd say: "You can't plough
a field by turning it
over in your head", leaving me
in no doubt as to what was work
and what wasn't.

Little did he know
how much I'd have given
to be able to live with the sound
the plough makes
in the loam, that peal
of cleave and turn
he could listen to and know
without the need to name it.

I have ransacked
whole languages for a word
that sound would inhabit,
a word strong and tender
as a hand stroking a breast,
a word which would bind together
the plough, the movement and the earth,
a word which would turn, Jack,
even your own head.

Haystacks

The storm waltzes them across the dark meadow
like shy dancers to the edge of the dance-floor,
their ochre frocks dishevelled, hair in straggles.

All night they strain under the wind's kiss
and come apart in the turgid, thunderous air.
It might be them and not the wind that moans.

You will find them the morning after
hanging to the tight wire of the fence,
broken as refugees at a closed border.

And nothing's left that's worth the saving
even with rural thrift. Their sodden forms molder
under the farmers' calculating eyes.

Not even the cattle will touch them.

II
Masque

Scrimshaw

What remains after so many huntings,
after the Arctic nights,
after the fat, brown women
who emerged laughing
into the lamplight
from chrysalis after chrysalis
of seal-skin and fur, what remains
after the plundered krangs
half submerged
like bleeding sores in the ice?

What girl would not lose her heart
to the man bringing back
the polished sperm-whale teeth
and the jaw-bones etched
with desire and tall tales
to be worn tight against her body
to perfect her shape
under new, red skirts?

The Catch

The image of the factory-owner's daughter
floats on the photograph's
sepia pool, an unfeminine
stance, feet planted wide apart showing
the outline of her long legs
under her dark dress.
Her hair is short
or tucked up under her narrow-brimmed hat.
She is smiling slightly
out of her broad and pretty face. Her
hands are placed firmly
on her hips, elbows sharp
even through her full, white blouse.
A shadow hides her eyes.

Your attention is caught
as much by what the girl is
standing on as by the girl:
the wide back of a half-
submerged Gray Whale
dead and roped to the dock.
A shadow on the water
could be a shadow
or a leak of blood.
In the background, too far
off to be distinguished
individually, a knot of workmen
lounges beneath a gigantic
letter O on the company's name-sign,
discussing the catch,
or the girl's abundant ass
pointed in their direction.

Epiphanies

I. Breughel's *Triumph of Death*, 1987

We have engineered ourselves a quiet place
far from the blinding nuclear blooms,
where our Decameron songs erase
the loud and pitiful finale
of a bloody history play.

At peace on the bed of her blue dress
I am blind to the accusing bones
marching to the rattle of vitrifying clay.
Let the mottled fools in some rat-king's court
screech tomorrow's epics about decay.

II. In Memory of Jackson Pollock

Traveler, having come clear
of jungles where
words like mosquitos swarmed and fed
on Reason's afterbirth,
you found not even ruined cities
whose hieroglyphic tombs
could intimate a life
we'd recognize.

So, you returned, cartographer
of an empty country
whose maps like Dark Age legends say:
Here be dragons, do not enter here,
while the virus you brought back
multiplies in our minds,
and in our fever
we hallucinate the real.

Rewind

Wing and thorn remain, etched into my mind;
images I choose for a leavetaking
in memory's montage. I rewind
the scenes we made when our lives were breaking.

Meeting you now, I take your offered hand,
forget the stark simplicity of pain,
buy you a drink, as a friend, you understand,
and after goodbyes wing and thorn remain.

Expecting too much, the expectation
projects the darkness of a tree bloomed bare.
How absence flits through the recreation
of such a photogenic, small affair.

Trapping

Sometimes I recognize the trace,
but more often than not
it is a strange, unimagined spoor
which brightens under my fingers,
and the sound, too, hanging
on the green dark, intimates beasts
far stranger than foxes,
more improbable than leopards.

Strange, too, that everything
can be used for bait—the feet I chopped
from an old man, photographs, concepts
even, hovering like bits of mist
over the gleaming teeth of the trap
and the shining, vocative O of the trigger—
no need to conceal the instrument:
what comes will come.

As for the waiting, it might be hours
or years. It is best, perhaps, to place
oneself in an old house with clear views
from all the windows, and trophies
emblazoned on the walls. What comes
will come, and there will be a shaking
among the trees, and then, not a cry
but a deep silence. The teeth mesh and hold.

Tale

I gather myself
around my own fire
as a man who has come in
from a dark scuffling of snow
to tell of his travels
through the tundra.

One year, I say,
I shot a buck
Coyote wanted for himself
which angered him so much
he walked me into
one of my own traps.

With my right foot twitching
in a pool of my own blood,
Take all the meat you want,
I yelled to him, just get me out!
And he did, though howling with laughter,
he let wolves track me all the way back.

You can believe what I say
is true by the way
my own shadow hunkers
closer to the fire, nodding as if
there are a thousand stories
to prove such things are always happening.

Without Design

The trees extend their lives in growing circles,
A solid sunlight burns inside each ring.
In crooked lines I grow as best I'm able.

Uncertainty and fear, these constant troubles
Define the deepest nature of my being.
While trees extend their lives in growing circles

I start and stop, change direction, struggle
To endings and then, once more, begin:
In crooked lines I grow as best I'm able.

I'm pushed to action by an inner muddle,
It isn't light but darkness makes me sing.
The trees extend their lives in growing circles -

I stumble through their shining forests, tremble
At what beats behind the perfect forms of things.
In crooked lines I grow as best I'm able,

Formless, unplanned, every move a gamble
Where I can't tell whether I lose or win.
The trees extend their lives in growing circles;
In crooked lines I grow as best I'm able.

Talking with Lions

The lions were astonished at first
when I came and lay down beside them
in the spikey, yellow grass,
on the plane tree's blue shadow.
They scrutinized me, politely,
for technologies (Machines
inhibit us, said a black-maned male)
and finding that I was clean
relaxed and grurrled a welcome.

A lioness talked about the hunt -
the pleasure of throbbing entrails
on the tongue, the antelope's warm body
writhing against her like a lover's,
(this, a lion-joke; lion-guffaws,
raw-meat-breath smell, heavy thwaks
of paws).
The oldest lion reminisced
(grumble-growls, same old stories)
about how sweet the tall hunters
of the savannah used to smell
(Aaah, fawn-blood-sweet!)
when he got up close, just to hear their songs...

And so we talked, yes, just so we talked
in the short grass under the plane tree.

But why, a young lion said to me,
have you...well...condescended (lion-titters)
after all this time to talk with us?

Brother, I said, my people spend their days
chattering with computers; they construct
gigantic metal ears to eavesdrop
on galaxies. I can't understand,
I said, their obsession. After all,
the wind blows singing from the pine-woods
and swallows bluster by with news
from Morocco. But my neighbours
sit listening to the television
telling them it has something to tell them
which it never tells them;
and no one speaks to anyone...

And so we talked, on into the night.
The moon came down and nested
in the plane tree. She smiled and whistled.

Remembrance

There were rumours of my fingers in Peru,
and traces of my tongue in Samarkand.
There were whispers of my veins in Timbuctoo,
and evidence of my bones in Swaziland.

From Swaziland the leopards brought my bones,
from Samarkand my tongue came on a leaf,
from Timbuctoo the spiders dragged my veins,
from Peru my fingers flew by condor's beak.

And I could feel the jungle in my fingers,
could taste the rolling plains upon my tongue,
and through my veins there coursed the winds of deserts,
tall grasses by fresh water filled my bones.

Across formations of forgetfulness
I pieced myself together bit by bit,
filling up the geographies of emptiness;
mapping my body, I remembered it.

Night Swimming

Lorraine would bring wild apples and I would bring
a lamp to read our faces by; the grass
was wiry and always damp on the steep hill
to the old reservoir, the only place
where we could be alone and swim those nights.
Was there a moon? Perhaps there was a moon,
since it was bright wherever we sat down
to undress each other like and unlike
lovers, lingering with our looks
over more variations of light and dark
than we thought possible in life or art.
There was a fearlessness in our flights
into the still, black water, the clasping
and unclasping of our bodies hardening
and softening, swimming into each other
until, breathless, we would drag ourselves
out over the weed-tangled rim to lie down.
Later I would slice the apples into halves,
pick the dark seeds out of the flesh-white fruit.
Lorraine would read in the lines of my hands poems
full of unfulfilled desires in the lamplight;
and my senses would close like oyster-shells
around the tart expectancy of it all,
and I wondered if this was the start of love
and why there would come suddenly to mind
images strong as memory, a Chinese landscape,
a boy with a lantern crossing a wooden bridge
to an island, a girl waiting under willow trees;
and the light he carried stayed after he
had passed on the trees, the water and the girl.
And Lorraine when she finished reading, would sigh,
get up, and pull me after her into
the glistening pool of night, the apples
bright as pearls on the wet, moonlit grass.

Jealousy

Love, the cat slinks
into our bedroom, kisses you fiercely,
insinuating his emery tongue
between your full lips, pausing
to cut me with the flick of his thin sneer
before disappearing.

Afterwards I have the Taxi-dream:
There are three of us—you, I,
and the tall man, his face smug, handsome
with continual accomplishment. We
step outside the mirrored lounge
of the bright hotel into the wet evening.
Taxi!", he calls out, and ushers you
fluidly into the immediate
waxed, black car. He joins you. I
am rooted to the ground, and as you leave
he smiles and tips his sleek fedora to my heart.

Love, our cat drags his catches
across the vegetable patch to his favorite
spot, often, a rabbit twice his size,
and I have seen him nuzzling industriously
in the bloody flocculence of the limp meat
clasped against his chest. "Yah!", I've shouted at him,
"Yah! Get away!". He raises his head and hisses,
flashing at me his huge, white, unscarable eyes.

An Honest Lie

Driven by loneliness and lust
to her pink
bed in Berlin,
"Ich liebe dich", I said,
knowing
that later I could blame
a defective phrase-book
and my ignorance of the language
for whatever wall
the words put up between us.

Tristia

There is no science of separation
to console us with inevitable ends.
Each parting makes its own lamentation.

I've stood in a dozen crowded stations
where crowds dissolved the faces of lovers, friends.
There never was a science of separation

to let me know the final destinations
of those trains: That open distance will not mend.
Each parting sings its own lamentation -

heart-splitting whistle, dark silence, passion
of tongue and touch, emptiness no emptiness portends.
There is no science of separation,

only things to clutch in desperation -
a tune, a certain look; it's always different:
Each parting spins its own lamentation,

and the stars in their inhuman isolation
don't burn with the fires our tattered hearts expend.
There is no science of separation.
Each parting flares its own lamentation.

Evolution Prayer

Dark night of my heart, raked
in the blizzard of my ten thousand lives,
I am again briefly
the Moloch of blind fish, sing again
briefly the pterodactyl's jubilas
to the sun, am sacrificed
again briefly for the dog's kingdom...
Dark night of my heart, I scream
in recollection of comfortless origins,
suffer for the arrogance
of my entropy. God protect me
from sins of stasis, keep me
in the movement that fixes me.

Meditation on an Incomplete Poem of Sappho

Because she is a woman the loss grows in us.
In this we are still snared by the legend of the Fall:
her poem, now, an icon of original absence,
and we, my brothers, tumescent with an excess of grief,
excess of the uncomprehending flesh hurting us onwards,
backwards, and driving us to shout for knowledge
in the very place of mystery.
                                                    It is possible
the word "love" spoken by a woman can stand alone,
can be love, and not require (in a man's words)
an object, being an absolute, like living,
and not a deprivation in the self which sends us
howling after completion; I do not know,
I do not know.
                                    But I remember once waking
suddenly in the night and seeing the rising moon
push such roses out of herself the woman beside me
burned and opened like a night-flower. And I knew
that entering her was an arrogance because of how she said
"I hope I am enough for you, I hope we won't be sorry",
and then we were.
                  Even so, there may be times when we can
                                                    know ourselves
to be complete; not perfect, but not, either,
the result and means of each other's salvation.
It may be enough that a poem of Sappho's
should begin with the word "soft"; that there is
emptiness among the names of gods, emptiness
among the actions of the hands, and at the end
the words "I shall come", the missing lines
no loss because not needed.
                                                    We should learn,

my brothers, there is nothing to restore,
that we come to each other as unexpected gifts,
as light cleaving to light, darkness to darkness,
unfallen, unredeemed, human;
and if we cannot explain ourselves to ourselves
neither can we blame. No words can cover
what we do not know.

She

Children, Home, Church: she is scourged at these three fat
pillars
of wisdom, condemned to wipe the arses of her kids,
to wipe the windows of her semi-detached prison cell,
to wipe the face of Christ and see the imprint doctored.
She is cut up and down to size, the extra inches
for her breasts come off the extra inches on her thighs;
her chin, too angular, is saved by a plastic insertion
tailored to suit her smile. And now that she's so pretty
no cause to spoil the surgeon's handiwork, to line her forehead
trying to safecrack the meanings of words she needn't know.
And when she takes to bed in the afternoon a box
of Valium and a bottle of gin, she's an ungrateful
bitch whose weeping husband gave her everything - children,
home
and love that was matched only by the love of God Himself.

The Circulation of the Light

I.

The dream comes so often I expect it now
the Tree-dream, the one with the flock of birds
and Roberto, and the bare tree
a wind is blowing through.

II

I wake earlier and earlier
to the summer sky's unforgiving blue,
a profusion of thrush-song and swift-song.

III

As boys we set traps
for starlings and wagtails, and when we had caught
a dozen or more we kept them
in wire mesh cages until night.
One by one we took them out, dipped their tails
in spirits and set them alight to watch
their brief flarings across the darkness.
Pain sang in the air and entered me.

IV

"The Light", Lao-Tzu says, "is easy to move
but difficult to stop". It flies beyond
the edges of our actions, gathers
the grief of things, returns,
and goes again. We grow heavy
with the gifts of light.

V

Roberto is a powerful man
in Salvador, handsome and urbane.
The peasants call him 'Blowtorch Bob'
because of his preferred method of seeking
knowledge at the feet of the poor.
I wrote him once, asking him to use
his influence to find a missing farmer
from near Metapan. He did not reply.

VI

In the dream I am hidden inside a tree,
or have grown into it,
since, when the wind moves through the branches
my bones grind against each other.

A man strides across a dark landscape.
It is Roberto and he is wrapped
in a cloud of burning birds. They flock
to the tree, singing, and I am engulfed
in fire and light and begin to sing
a pain that is not my own.

Roberto sits beneath. His blowtorch howls.
I watch him turn it on his own bare feet.

No-Man

"No-man's treachery, No-man's violence is
doing me to death." (Odyssey, Bk. IX)

...he begins nowhere and ends nowhere;
graves are his footprints, systems, his shadows.
It is he who sends you sadnesses in Autumn,
who tells you that love is a kind of murder,
who tempts you with paradises. *Imagine yourself,*
he whispers, *standing outside the shock, shear
and drag of time; imagine the sumptuous
plenitude of "is", unending, painless.*
He swims behind your face in mirrors
and old photographs, floats up through the eyes
of your children. *Lie down,* he murmurs,
for your true destiny is sleep. Since
he disdains histories, he delights in History:
He is the emperor of categories,
the smile on the guards' lips as the trains
arrive at the death camp. He is No-man —
he is Man, abstract, murderous, actual,
beginning nowhere and ending nowhere...

Webs

How many degrees below freezing point
did it take to turn the webs on the cypress

to such a profusion of tattered silk
stalled in time, like Miss Havisham's wedding dress,

sequinned with black spiders and poked through
by a million green needles, the tree's memories?

III

West

Redwoods

The redwoods gather to themselves only
the choicest winds, the kinds that make you

go silent to be certain that what you hear
is the movement of air through branches

and not the low persistent whisperings
of another. To walk by yourself in redwood groves

can turn your mind like nothing else.
Try as you might to see them

only as trees striking conclusively
for that part of the air where the sky begins,

their easy interweaving in that rare space
makes you think of the lives you almost shared

where breezes may just as well have been storms
for the damage you caused as you weathered them.

Anishinabemowin

the language of the Chippewa Indians —
I'd have had to invent it myself
if it didn't exist, just to cope
with the way I dream your home to be,
a continent of sounds unknown to me,
as I trace my finger through lakes and plains
and finally lie low in Omaha.

Last night I dreamt we lay under bearskins
while the snowdrifts of Minnesota
mountained over us in the darkness.
They were like dream-animals, dark and shapeless,
shifting and howling in the ceaseless winds.
"Takatam!", said the avalanche that set us running.
And we lay low, we lay low in Omaha.

Once, red-eyed from a thousand miles of highway,
croaking songs from Shakespeare's plays (*O mistress mine...
Come unto these yellow sands...*) I saw your hands
white-knuckled on the steering wheel turning us
through towns whose sounds I was almost drunk on.
"Tashawa!", you said, doing a mental rain-dance,
till we lay low, we lay low in Omaha.

Anishinabemowin, the language
of the Chippewa Indians, comes to mind
as a low rumble under the straight lines
of asphalt and cut stone. I'd have had to invent
it myself just to cope with each turn in the road
that leads to where I dream your home to be,
through a continent of sounds unknown to me,

stopping nightly to lie low in the long, deep O
that calls inside the name of Omaha full stop.

In Light of Kansas

It strikes you suddenly,
the way the deserted light
in one of those Hopper paintings
ambushes you with unspeakable grief,
how instinct shades into purpose.

Next month, the boy is telling you
as he pumps your gas, he
and his girl will be married. The paint job
on the red Chevy? Yep, it's all
his own work and not bad, eh?

You accelerate from the place
and the idea as the sky begins
to bruise the blue out of itself,
but fifty miles further through the flat land
you're back again, and then again.

Filling stations and motels
happen and unhappen in the dusk,
and in these neon arenas
you catch sight of the boys leaning
against the inevitable

pick-ups and girls.
You cannot stop
thinking how each is the other's
unintended accomplishment, necessity
blurred into love and decision.

In the middle of nowhere
you stop your car, turn the lights off
and sit there in the dark.
The sky bristles with stars
and from the black fields

you hear insects sawing messages
from their own bodies.
Hours later you will check in
at one or another Diner & Motel
where the drained waitress will tell you

sure, why not, she'll spend the night,
though she'll never know what
it meant, all that odd talk
about the dark and light
grinding down Kansas between them.

Home Sickness

The logging-road of my sadness
winds all the way to Belfast

through hills of stumps and ashes
and the fractured bones of saplings.

A scrub-jay screeches from a clutch of weeds
like something wounded left for dead.

II.

The woman was left as a warning, tied
to the gates of a church. A hysterical
sign beside her screamed BRIT LOVERS BEWARE.

They'd stripped her naked, shaved her crotch and head,
leaving a raw scuff of bluish stubble.
On her breasts, the intimate bites of cheap cigars.

III.

The logging-road of my sadness
begins and ends in Belfast,

winds through the blasted, clear-cut streets
past children smashing abandoned trucks.

A wino slumped in a doorway roars
at invisible tormentors.

Mrs. America

Fearful of becoming their own images,
the movies blessed them with the means to self
deception: Norma-Jean-pouts, a grammar
of hips and hair; each movement baited
to tempt John Wayne, or a private (first class)
who'd tell them "Yah, the war was just like that".
But frailty's true name is forty-nine,
pleasure a paunched and sweaty rarity,
Norma-Jean like every goddess dies
and soldier husbands booze and fade away,
leaving a million Helens staring into mirrors,
their wrinkled reflections launching back to them
desires like doomed ships coming across a sea
whose calmness is the poise of ambush.

The Impersonators

She wakes up far too early
leaving her latest lover for Dostoevsky.

When she scrambles through chapter two
of The Idiot she hears noises from below herself.

Pushing thirty, the seven year
leprosy of becoming another Marilyn

is scaring off her closest friends
with the stench from her perfumed wounds.

Another matinee without one unmangled line
and she lets herself be fucked into oblivion

by someone who'll join in her pretense
that she's a goddess and he's the President.

Whales in October
For Kate

Let me imagine myself back to the time
when "whale" is a preacher's word breaching
the tense, gray light of the soul's ocean,
and uncharted island, harbour
to such thoughts as gannet the hours of sleep.
Understand, then, the pilgrimage of the hunt,
the chasing of the word become dark flesh
among the featureless ice-floes, God's
own blood pulsing in the arm slinging the harpoon,
the slurring kiss of the hit: It is
a religious act, repentence of a kind,
and from it light comes into the world.

Now it is October and Oregon.
The first whales are moving along the coast,
outriders of the yearly migration, slow
because they are the first and the season young.
I have read they are related to deer
and antelope, of their great tenderness
toward each other, their songs.
"Whale", now, might be the word
a singer would sing at a time when the flesh
is a continuous light of its own making,
as when a man and woman take each other
in their arms and are no longer in pain
because no longer alone and alone.

This too would be a mistake. Is not
everything adequate to itself, a fullness

beyond naming except to say it is
what it is and not another? Today
I watched the whales traveling, green forms
driving through the green ocean, rising
to spout and breathe the crisp October air,
and I know it is enough, it is enough.

IV

A Wren

A Wren

Up an hour, and the sun
scarcely high enough to clear
the line of the near hills.

The clean, sweet gum of alder sap
threw an invisible halo
around the pile of newly split logs.

I sat on the chopping-stump,
rested my chin on the maul's shaft,
watched spider-strings hang in the gray air.

It was not growing weather
nor the time of rot, this pallid March
with the snow in the sky.

A wren fluttered clumsily
from a tangle of roots
to the milky pith of the stacked logs.

He prised out grubs
with quick, jerky stabs of his beak,
fearless, a foot away.

I described him to myself
to relieve my head
of its clog of hard dreams,

noted with pleasure
four blended shades of brown
in his ruffling feathers.

I stood to resume my work;
the bird made a low, ungainly flight
behind some rocks.

I cleaved the maul through a log,
relished the crisp snap of the two halves
parting, falling perfectly away.

In the house my wife was singing;
from the chimney
a flourish of smoke.

The wren reappeared, dark eye
glistening. I knew if I could touch him
I would burst into flight and song.

At the Black Edge

Our arms have grown
deep and wide as snowfields,
covering everything, drawing the trees, the stars,
the deer and the tall cities around us.
It is too much
for them to bear, and we
who demand such close knowing
we approach the atom
to explain the mountain. Already we see
the gods taking flight like a cloud of swallows,
their homes which are horses, and fish, and fish-
hooks becoming hard and pale as jewels
in our embrace. At the black edge
of the world two or three flowers are tossing
in the approaching blizzard of our words.
We cannot hear them singing
above our exquisite howl.

About the Author

Ger Killeen was born in Limerick City, Ireland, in 1960. He was educated at the local Christian Brothers School and at University College Dublin where he won prizes in Literature and Philosophy. His work has appeared in a number of periodicals in Ireland and in this country, including *New Irish Writing, Tocsin, The Limerick Poetry Broadsheet, The News Guard,* and in *Construction Ahead,* Sparrow Poverty Pamphlet #56. He came to the United States in 1987 and is now married and living at Neskowin, on the Oregon coast.